To Origin

Also by Greg Tome and published by Ginninderra Press
Watching from the Shadows
Tilting at Time

Greg Tome

To Origins and Back

Thanks

My thanks to Anna Kerdijk Nicholson, Peter Lach-Newensky,
Anthony Mills, Rhiannon Hall and Van Ikin for their
continual support and guidance.

I also acknowledge the members of the poetry subgroup of the
Southern Highlands branch of the Fellowship of Australian Writers
for their support. I am indebted to Greg Baker and Uta Purcell,
as leaders of the Southern Highlands branch,
for their unstinting encouragement.

To Norma, Matthew and Erica

To Origins and Back
ISBN 978 1 76109 359 3
Copyright © text Greg Tome 2022
Cover image: Matthew Tome

First published 2022 by
GINNINDERRA PRESS
PO Box 3461 Port Adelaide 5015
www.ginninderrapress.com.au

Contents

Verbatim

Sharper than any knife
softer than any blanket
stronger than any chain
gentler than any kiss

In the hands of the wrong leader
        more dangerous
                than any bomb

Used wisely and with good intent
        more healing
                than any balm

The building blocks of communication
The rungs to higher thought
The alpha and omega of relationship

Sporting more hooks than any virus

So many
        changing
                dynamic
                        restless
                fierce
        cool

        WORDS

2B or other

I lean on sticks
        little regular sticks
                coloured red and black
        in longitudinal stripes
with dark pointy ends

Pencils bear me up
        2B to 6B
                guide my hand
        in sensuous exercise
gliding across the welcoming embrace
        of generous white paper

I write anything
        complaints   plans
                nonsense sentences
Sometimes
        a delicate seedling of thought emerges
        needing to be removed
                to a safer area
There hopefully to thrive
        mature into a fully formed poem

Pencils set aside
        after this yearned-for morning ritual
                my psyche leans back
                        looks around
                            and
                                  smiles

The first Thursday

Following the graceful stream
                of lunar dance
on a day named for the old thunder deity
we meet
        in this unlikely temple
                where squashed-up white walls
absorb

                images   rhythms   touching memories
        flashes of anger   unspoken love
        words aching to touch the face of some god

So much
        one fears the saturated surfaces
                must one day yield
        with poetry trickling down
           in silent tribute
        to the warm bond –
                caffeine-steamed –
        that presses us together
The visceral reachings-out of each
        savoured   pondered   cherished
                        by all
Such sharing a generosity
        that sits in a territory
                far away from the everyday

We leave
    we trail the moon
        through seven- day allotments
    until it's time
        to re-gather
    enchanted by the prospect
        more poetry
           more sharing

Grammarian to his love

If only I were able
       to fondle your subjunctive
to feel your infinitive against my body
while savouring the gentle breath
           of your present participle
Let my hands caress your imperative mood
Long have I desired your perfect tense

But always I am rejected
        by your passive voice

Thoth – then and now

All the scribes of old Egypt
       carved out stately hieroglyphs
       declaiming to the world from temples
           monuments   statues
Scribes recorded in hieratic
           officialdom's needs
Others scratched their demotic
           into personal letters   diaries
All were beholden to him
       the hooked-beak long-step strutting bird
           the ibis
       Thoth
           the god of writing

Millennia later
       the spawn of his writing
              lives on
Hieroglyphs nestle in the smart phone cameras
              of countless tourists
Papyrus pieces cosset in museums

Thoth the god of writing reigns
              no more
       his ibis form has fallen
              on hard times
       scavenging through city park rubbish bins
              across the globe

The skill of writing no longer
                              the right of a chosen few
The gratifying motion
                    of directing pen or pencil
            yields great territory to the finger tapping
                    on the keyboards
of myriad puzzling devices
                    that broadcast creativity
                              into an absorbent ether
            Gems and trash abound

Thoth's abandoned throne
            now warmed by the buttocks
                    of another Egyptian deity
Seth
            the god of Chaos

Infants School Playground

A chaos of mice they scamper
                    in all directions
Their laughter
        squealing
                create moments sealed off
        from
                envy   fright   spite
        from any sense of care

The sight of their hats
                wide floppy brims
        their subtly varied uniforms
        brand them as tribal members

In adult life will they remember
        this purity in fierce energy
        this uncritical acceptance of life?

If only there were some machine
                able to freeze-frame such moments
        slide them into adult lives
                hard   clear   unchanging

Boyhood memory

A solitary boy
        wandered the stretches
        of featureless paddocks
thoughts running around
        in his head
            unpredictably
many arising from the entrails
        of the one-roomed box-shaped school
            within easy walking distance
                down the road

He wondered
        what crocodiles look like up close
        or the shape of earthquakes
With a stick he decapitated thistle heads
        imagined he was slaughtering Japanese soldiers
        his random musings drifting through the air
        after the thistledown

There was a mystery about girls
        such as his nearby cousins

            or

What was it like to be grown-up
        or in another country
            such as where the Eskimos lived
To be old
        like Old Ted
            whose house was there
        on the horizon
            lazy chimney smoke
                marking its existence

Old Ted
       with his bent-stem pipe
            knobbly walking stick
and four or five word answers
       to every question he posed to him –
life's complexities wool-pressed
       into a small simple box

He ruefully eyed the eroded gully
       where once a wasp he disturbed
          stung him fiercely
          about the neck
       sending him bawling all the way
       back to the house

Back to the house now
               he decided
to help carry afternoon tea
up to the shearing shed
perhaps to be given one or two
       recently cooked biscuits

In his own old age
       he revisits the memory
          of the solitary boy
       and as much as he can
          of time since
       his thoughts shaping delta-like
       fanning wide long
               shallow

leading him to tread an eggshell path
to that great sweep of experience
seeking meaning
finding none

Brief early morning moments

He sits on the side of the bed
                    trying to belch
The fluorescent numbers from a clock brand
                    2.36   across the skin
          of the young morning hour
Close by
          his sleeping wife's uneven breathing distracts
                              disconcerts
The silence in the great mouth of night
          tolerates the courting sounds of a lone train
                              ringing out
                    as it woos the stoic station
He shrugs
          sips water
                    gathers his insignificance about him
                    clambers back between the warming sheets
There he contemplates
          unimportance   false hopes   daily routines

          Wonders if there is anything else

Life shrinks

All that matters
        whether the postman has delivered
            the next power bill
        what the bank balance shows
        what the columnist has written
            about that politician
        what we have for dinner
        who the last episode
                reveals to be the killer
        what the temperature will be
            if there's another tomorrow

Her way

Strong skinny old
her heart beats in rhythm
with birds and trees
She lives her way

Walking with a group
through the summer heat bush
beside a big river
a halt is called

Gently stooping trees
pour succour and shade
onto all recumbent walkers
all but her

She slips out of her clothes
she slips into the water
which recognises a kinship
granted to only a few

On land again
she flourishes a handkerchief
across the narrow tracts
of wet skin

Soon dressed
she continues a part
of the walking group
Continues to live her way

Double Tetractys

Hands
are fine
for holding
showing your love
as well as all the other things they do
mostly for the good we hope but beware
when one becomes
a clenched
fearsome
fist

Sound
shaped
with great skill
as harmony
will become music in its many forms
classic being the most influential
across the world
for those who
dare to
dream

Circular Quay on Anzac Day

The march long finished
    a few of its suited bemedalled relics
        linger with the larger crowd
    today their backs are straighter
        than on other days
    most now with ties removed

For everyone else life surrounds
        where the sun flirts outrageously
    with the seductive harbour waters

The young bare their limbs brazenly
    to hoodwink summer
        to loiter for a few more weeks
So many desirable women
    so many dorky male companions

An occasional ferry
    furrowing up its self-importance
        a preliminary act to another parade
        another set of uniforms
    a line of Buddhist monks
    pose a different set of questions

Frequently heard ventral didgeridoo notes
    absent this day
Busked electric guitar fails
    to measure up

Families from near
          from faraway lands
     share prized shaded benches
          share smiles nods of gratitude
Politeness spilt in all directions

Differences in appearance
          in language
     countered by the uniformity
               of cardboard boxes
          from which all extract the fuel
     needed for the afternoon
          and whatever it might bring

Into the fray with LBJ

Side by side we press our backs
               into the road's unfriendly surface
Both hands each hold
               that of a neighbouring stranger
For the time being not a stranger
                        but a fellow warrior
Lyndon Johnson's plane has landed
          his car headed this way
The back seat accommodates Johnson   his ego
          and sycophant Askin
Run over the bastards sets the tone
Police seize my ankles
          drag me groundwise to a van
My back bleeds   I lose a shoe
Nothing compared to a napalm bath
                        or a sniper's bullet

History marks down the Vietnam War
               Johnson's grim aim not to be the first
                        of his kind to lose a war
My back heals a few proud scars remain
I buy new shoes   a new shirt
History says little about those who struggled but failed

Ours is the sad compensation of being right
               but futile in challenging the great wrong

Forged in anger

The fierce glare from the furnace a jolt
                to his face and shoulders
      the heat
                a wall pushing against his shovelling arms
He wills the allocated bites of coal
          into the gluttonous fire
Pain sprints through the byways
                of his body
Coal dust and sweat combine
                to paint his bare torso
      his face
Excess soot infiltrates his ears
                nostrils
      comic masks his eyes
                wet mouth
In his heart
          forged by the heat
      a steely anger at this penance
          having to help propel this troopship
              across the soupwarm sea
                  to where war awaits
Some relief when a fellow digger
              takes possession of shovel
The cooling steel-shaped anger remains

The stench of battle chokes him
  fear tears at his throat
Confusion abounds from the high-speed chaos
Loving concern for flashy chestnut Toby
  sweaty spirited partner
    he rides into combat day after day
      lodges

   alongside scorn for officers
   aping English counterparts
    showing no concern
  for the likes of him
    or Barney
      or Slip
        or Jack
          or Darkie

Senselessness torments him
  trying to kill men he doesn't know
  well enough to hate

In quiet times with his gang of five
  or what's left of them
    tightly bonded soulmates
  closer than any brothers could be
    the flavour of mateship covers over
  but never eradicates
    the barb of anger in his heart
Why me?
  Why here?
    Why this?

Decades later
                eyeing his brood of sons
            sees no troopship stokers
                no lighthorse soldiers
                            surviving the desert hardships
Doughboys all he pronounces

At times
        the anger forged so long ago
                breaks through the cultivated crust
                            of loving fatherhood
Why not them?
        Why me?

He fights to recognise this part of his nature
        fails to understand it
This fires his anger all the more

The slovenly youngest son
        earns a kick up the backside
                for leaving off the wet wheatbag
                        cooling the soft drink bottles
        there for some family function

Old age pretends to mellow
        but resentment continues
                ferrets its way into times spent
        staring into space
                seeing nothing
                        re-seeing everything
                replaces much treasured Toby
        from the never forgotten years
                by carrying him forward
        from one day
                into the next

Returned man

He lies on his side
        propped up on one elbow
lies across a part of the bowling green
        plucking out invasive weeds
                testing the chastity
                        of the sacred turf
turf to be scrutinised by keen-eyed men-in-white
        whose week spills over
                into Sunday arvo bowls
        and such comments
                It's playin' a bit quick today, Jack
For them
        his is gentle work
        suitable for a returned POW
        but it allows time to think
Time to remember capture
        befuddled commanders
                betrayed locals
                in disastrous Crete campaign
        dreamed up by woop-brained Churchill
        remember Stalag
                the failed attempts at escape
                        by acclaimed tin-legs hero
                reaping a bitter reprisal on all
the work building roads
        a futile gesture by a regime
trying to forestall the inevitable

Memories that scorch his stomach

Time to feel the tug of earth
reaching up through the grass
      measuring his body
      previewing a future all-encompassing embrace

Now
      this work here
      this life here
          in this gentle town
      like a diet of jelly
      flavour gone
          substance lacking

Yesterday
      a workmate with a not so different history
      searching for an answer to the emptiness
          fed his week's wages through the pokies
Management re-paid
          counselled   threatened
      Jelly prevailed

      After work today
          home to steadfast wife
              inquisitive son
There to find a greater purpose
      avoid stomach anguish
      avoid seeing his pain
          reflected in their eyes
      to seek some substance
          some sort of flavour
      for the jelly

Requiem for Friedrich Staps

In 1809 a young man seeks to kill Napoleon
His letter to parents
     – his father a pastor –
God has commanded me...
Turns his back on work at Erfurt
     (Martin Luther studied there
        another God man aiming to set the world right)
Turns his back on his love Margueritte
     she abhors you he later tells Napoleon *as much as I do*

Crusades his way over nine days to Austria
     too late by minutes to use a first Vienna opportunity
God gives strength of patience to believers
Eight autumnal days float by
     on the buoyancy of Friedrich's purpose

Schonbrunn Palace a muscular flaunting
     of Hapsburg megalomania
     suits Bonaparte's choice for reviewing a parade
Friedrich is there
     fondling a kitchen knife that aches
        to engage with the rarest flesh which rules
        his beloved people
     and which befouls the German race

Among petitioners only Friedrich insists
     on speaking to the Emperor
God gives him courage
     but fails to add cunning

A sense of stony purpose
                    leaves no room for canny trickery
Suspicion leads to search
                    leads to arrest
            to confession of intent freely given

This occasion sees one life saved
            with many hundreds of thousands
                    fated to be lost over the next six years
But kill the Emperor
Why?

Friedrich refuses to answer
                    unless Bonaparte is present
Bewildered that anyone would wish to harm
                    the paragon of Western enlightenment
            Napoleon obliges

The imperial presence fazes the prisoner
                    not at all
Friedrich treats his inquisitor as an equal
                    but with politeness
The naked honesty of succinct answers
            befuddles Napoleon unused to such qualities
                    from underlings
More disconcerting
            a doctor's analysis
                    Friedrich is sane and healthy

A conditional offer of a pardon
    I will still try to kill you

Four days later
    still unfazed
        having refused to eat tyrant's food
    his eyes glance along the row
        of firing squad's muskets
      pointing his destiny
    Too many to count

He punches the air
      mouths his defiance
    Long live freedom!
    Long live Germany!
    Death to this tyrant!

So many similar calls repeated
      through time
    over and over
      wafted away on the wings of futility
    to fade somewhere in the ether
      always accompanied by the spit of rifle shots

Ophelia drowning

based on a painting by John Millais

Above the water surface
                hands implore the still air
      her pale face mouths words
                  from yearning songs
     she lies afloat the gentle stream
The water boosts the bold peacock-tail colours
                 of her defiant dress
     doomed soon to surrender to saturation
            drag its contents
                down   into
                        another world
    where the edgy tensions
        of Elsinore court
           do not exist
   nor the mind-splitting
                heart-splitting clash of loves
      for father and prince
   for father killed by prince

Streamside
     flowers   leaves reflect
            the prince's elusive   flickering love
    the father's love
             in the branches
        menacing   protecting
   reaching over that vulnerable face
            framed by her wayward floating hair

Away from this idyllic stream
      to a gaping resting place in a graveyard
In contrast to the peace
         of where she yielded up her life
     pyrotechnics will reign
        as grieving brother
            and guilt-ridden lover
        challenge abuse posture
     Braggadocio threats insults
       split the air

So many words
       too late
   Far

     too
        late

Behind the mask of the Queen of Naples

based on Jean Auguste Ingres portrait of Caroline Murat

A stately dramatic pose
  uncomfortably trying to replicate my brother-consul's earlier portrait

in striking fashionable black
                      camouflaging my swirling doubts

feathered headgear resembling a warrior's helmet
                      married to a daredevil soldier-king

Steadfast large dark eyes
  gut-pained by Joachim's past long absences in Napoleon's army

in a patrician watch-your-step Corsican face
                      Napoleon confined to Elba isle

Regal trappings furniture drapes carpet all around
                      anti-Bonaparte forces muscling up

Behind her back the windowed Bay of Naples spreads its beauty
                      Vesuvius gushes a sullen smoky augury

Proud of Joachim's lifting Naples out of its feudal past
  terrified by the risks as he strives to be king of a united Italy

Defiantly challenging the future
                      fighting back my forebodings for the coming year

when her husband – king will be captured and shot
when her brother-protector will feel the lash of Waterloo

Strange fruit: different types, different places

Long before Billie Holiday angel-voiced the spectacle
        of trees boundaring southern USA
                while bearing strange black fruit
                        with twisted mouths
                                and bulging eyes –

Long before   in that same country
        an aberration trumpeted its way into power
personified by faux hair arrangement
        wimpy hand gestures
                grating words floating on a grating voice
                and a definite disdain for strange fruit kin –

Long before all that
        we had smeared unspeakable shame
                        across our vast landscape
        not fruit
                        but also black
                                more vegetable
        introduced to the soil
                        by whiplash of rifle shot
Too many to be buried by their own kind
        composted by time
                by nature
                        and conveniently faulty memory

Periodic exposures of such barbarism
        peeled back as from an onion
                left too long in the ground
        and guilt passed around like a disowned smelly parcel

Indigenous memory persists their story
    honours it with dance
       with written words
with Gurrumul
       with Archie Roach leading a people
   in soul-searing song that crosses an ocean
     to clutch at Billie's hand

Backyard rebirth

It might look ordinary to some
But there's an interesting array of shrubs
        arranged with nonchalant elegance
With different muscle power
        layers of overlapping greens
          caress the eye
A dominant yellow box eucalyptus or two
    a couple of different acacia types
No wretched northern hemisphere lawns here
Native grasses state their case
      everything native
Makes this backyard different
    but not extraordinary

There are times when the extraordinary
        can be sensed
A barefoot walk over this ground
      earns a shiver
         felt ascending the soil
Generations of stamping Gundungurra feet
          assert themselves

A burning smell
        claws at the air
        a campfire
     wild flesh smothered in hot ashes
Slender black children
      run   squeal   dodge
      throw thin sticks
         would-be spears

Women sit in a circle
            stitching skins
                        won from the bodies of possums

The power of the ages lasts only so long
The here-and-now look of the backyard space
            clamps down on the imagination
For now
            just a different
                        but not extraordinary
            backyard

Butcher-bird ritual

The soft feathery bundle
    a puffed-up body
        requesting sustenance
    at first glance
        vulnerable
but note ˊ
    the hook end of beak
the quick eye ensuring absence
    of competitors
        magpies
            mynahs
Confident in its superior speed
        it waits
    a handful of quivering energy
        perched on the back
            of an outdoor chair

I have been summoned by its song
    a mellifluous response
        to the parting of blinds
Aldi's vintage cubed
        into two bird-size servings –
    often a companion or offspring accompanies –
Today just a sole recipient

Door opens
    tiny body tenses
        squats
Cheese cube floats parabolically
        above the creature

It springs up to ballet a perfect catch
   before skimming low across yard
      over a fence
     to the comfort of home
I watch it disappear

For a breath or two
   I'm no longer an on-call flunky
More
  a loving
    beneficent god

Blackbutt Reserve, Newcastle, on a scorching hot day

The heat wraps all into a unity
    the surrounds
        native animals
            human visitors

Numerous lithe-bodied children
    are the least affected
        confidently immersed in pursuits
    that bedevil those accompanying –
mothers
    smoothly bare-legged
grandparents
    sensibly clad against the sun
fathers
    dressed as though skipping work

Peacocks strut around with casual hauteur
    reminding everyone of their rank
        with raucous calls that crack
            the calm of subservient trees
            and the surrounds
    momentarily halt the children
        attract their intense interest
            which dims just as quickly
Peacocks seek food from visitors
    without any hint of begging
    more like kings demanding taxes from subjects

Out of sight to all
        except those prepared to challenge
           the heat-laden ascent
    to where among the trees
        enclosures purport to be homes
    for a who's who of Australian wildlife

Visitors are greeted by the backsides of wombats
        their other ends head down and feeding
Emus inspect the same visitors
    confusing all as to who
            is visiting who

Wallabies keep their distance
           with elegant disdain

From the tiniest wren
        to the largest cockatoo
    an array of colourful birds
        flaunt their attractiveness
    because
        what else is there to do
    on a day like this?

Sensitive to its reputation
        of being a bit of a freak
    the platypus hides away
           as best it can

Storing up for their forays
        reptiles sprawl across a battery of rocks
                soaking energy from their surfaces
        bearded dragon
                lace monitor
                        diamond python

The most telling comment on the day
        comes from the koalas
                who set a shining example
        sleeping away the troublesome hours
                                of fierce heat

Tanka

Layers of verdure
stretching across all I can see
bring each day alive
with the belief beauty lives
and joyous calm can thrive

Not even trying
impossibly beautiful
outside the glass door
unaware of their impact
fuchsias in their pots hold sway

Istanbul visited

The booming voices of men
                        from other lands
            helps confound those pausing
                        over hotel breakfast choices
In the street
            short   strong   Turkish men
            friendly   beckoning
                        Eat my place
                        buy my goods
An old man pushes a cart
            calls out his wares
                        in a worn voice
Another man hoses the street
                        his head suited for the face of a coin
The jangle of trams answers
                        the call to prayers
Minarets challenge the sky
                        as fishermen line Bosphorus shores
            under the gaze of the Galata Tower
                        as they have for centuries

I am a stranger
                        there is too much history
            soaked into so many monuments
                        too many stories
The world flocks here to wonder
                        to be bewildered
            to stamp its incomprehension
                        into countless photographs

Too much to know
           to understand
It can be absorbed only
           through the pores of the skin
      only through the intake of breath

When that happens
    Here
    I am home

Desert days

Like palm trees randomly scattered
                    around an oasis
groups of men
            critical of the leadership
                    the stagnation
            mutter quietly   intensively
out of mouths hidden behind hands
            faces sideways
                    eyes swivel
Tattered dirty garments
            long tangled   hair   beards
                        smell of unwashed bodies
                neglect-coated teeth
            add to their unease
Scarce water enough only to drink
            wives wash crucial areas
            the rest used for cooking
Food measured out with overwhelming care
            healthy   regular   unchanging   then boring
            criticised
                    despite being a gift
            from some reluctant source

Stuttering old Moses
                    leans on his brother
            Aaron the eloquent
The second-hand messages
                    don't always cut through

Unsettled women look to some other source
      the ephemeral Miriam
           the ruling family's female
      signals occasional comfort

Moses goes missing
           climbing some impossibly steep hill
      summoned by an interfering CEO
While the cat's away
           the mice get restless
They want entertainment
      a sense of direction
    something to believe in
      to worship
Aaron senses the mood
      elicits some gold
    women's earrings   other jewellery
      grabbed from Egypt
    before the hurried exit
Builds a golden calf
    It does the trick

Their brains hammered
      by extensive periods of emptiness
    they fall to their knees
as they grasp to their hearts
      something precious
    special   solid   real

Miriam seems to have failed the test
                of seeing danger here
        warning caution to her brother
Plague and slaughter as inevitable
        as the daily delivery of manna

A younger man stands in the edge of the crowd
                    listening carefully
Speech problems and all
        Moses reads words
                inscribed on two stone tablets
Replacement copies
            after Moses smashed the originals
        in a dazzling display of anger
The youth hears the lists of forbidden covets
        wonders why they loom so large in the light
        of so many decades of desert life
        where privacy doesn't exist
            sharing is the norm
He can't help noticing the wife
            of a couple
        often his night-time neighbours
He allows himself one last covet
        long   slow   detailed
before the offence becomes firmly established

Randomly scattered groups of men
        stand discussing the more congenial terrain
Their voices loud
             clear
       their manner at ease with the novelty
          of signs of some greenery
       the occasional collection of cloud
They discuss the dead Moses
          they praise
               they question
They shrug their shoulders
      wave their arms
           agree   disagree
     compromise

The future beckons
        with headstrong Joshua to lead the way
The choice of Moses
        endorsed by the Controller
destined to lead them
        to the three-days'-march-away promised land
now the focus of hard-eyed survivors
            of the desert years

Their opinions range widely
       resembling the scatter of a sower's seed
       an image plucked from the dreams of each
       as he sees himself farming his own precious piece
          of milk-and-honey land

As ardent as their speculations
        they come nowhere near to foreseeing
                the ferocity of the seizure of the land
        destined to be theirs
                from the array of previous owners
        all the handiwork of Joshua's Commander-in-Chief

Or

        the staunching of the flow or River Jordan
        so these same men walk safely across its bed

Or

        the drama ending with the collapse of Jericho's walls

           All in the onrushing future

Buoyed by their optimism
            by their escape from desert life
        from close confinement with dispirited wives
            their predictions prove hopelessly astray

Long they stand
        peppering the air with untethered words

Mountainous aspirations

Some mountains aren't yet mountains
Mount Gibraltar an example
           too small to be a mountain
                     while hosting a pretentious name
Making a reasonable job
                          of being a pretend mountain
           it survives close to its original state
                     with an abundance of native trees
                              fringing rocky cliff faces
           a muscular glowering presence
           guarding the northern approach to the town
                     snuggling into its sheltered valley
These days the Gib displays modest mountain features
           trains humiliated into the innards of a tunnel
           radio signals and similar hampered
                     in their arrogant colonisation of the ether
In times past mountains have thrust up outlandishly
                     into the welcoming air above
           while discarded others sank from view
One day Mount Gibraltar might look
           from much higher up at the rest of the world
Before then a name change beckons
                     Bowrell
           its original Gundungurra title
                          ideal

South of Tamworth

Far away in the distance
        away back in the lap of time
I remember different hills
        shaped as if by gods
                goddesses of classical times
stretching away as far as possible
snuggling under an aura of beauty
            purring at the colours
                embroidered into them

I remember towns that sing intriguing names
        Murrurundi
                Currabubula
                        Wallabadah
Quirindi
        and to balance the aesthetic
        Willow Tree

Each hosts a desperation of signposts
        of varied hues

      SCHOOL   POLICE
           RSL   SALVATION HALL
AMBULANCE
                CEMETERY

I remember
          titan-shaped muscular edifices
                    that challenge the sky
          as they baby-sit the abundant produce
                    from surrounding land

I remember other buildings
                    quasi museum discards
          tired old darlings that have lost their looks
                    which no amount of tarting up
                              can ever restore

Contemporary sleek numbers
                    sit randomly scattered
          all their glitter failing to overcome
                    sense of inappropriateness

I wonder about bright-eyed men and women
          plucked from faraway larger centres
                    from close parental contact
          to long-range parental concern
                    taking up tasks in these towns
as
          teachers   nurses   police
                    other ancillary workers
The questions posed
                    where to live
          who to love
                    how to wrestle the beckoning leisure hours
          how to process the unfamiliar landscape
                    a challenging Attica
          reeking of empty agelessness

But it's the hills that stamp the over-riding character
                    of this region
          south of Tamworth
It's the hills
          more artfully arranged than the many breasts
                    in the echoing image of
                    Artemis of Ephesus
          created
                    so far away
                              so long ago
                    but well after these hills

                    It's the hills

To origins and back

I drive north
        to where my brothers' bones
                my parents' bones
        enrich the earth that blankets them
I drive past hefty hills
        wrestling with their individual shapes
past clusters of trees competing
        to claim the sky

I emerge from sloping eastern lushness
        to a bleached flatness that insists
                on shrivelled trees
        scattered across grandmotherly paddocks
Empty-eyed cattle gather forlornly
        where food will arrive eventually

Further on
        different paddocks
                different contents
        huge granite boulders lie
            where they were spewed up
                by a volcano
        eons ago

Then the town
        where so much of it began
        so much has ended
Weighed down by its Scottish title
        it attaches itself to the lining
            of a languid river's valley

Now a centre
     whose unrelentingly regular matrix
     absorbs from far afield
an influx of pilgrims
       linked by kinship

Names
     greetings
        embraces
           laughter
              warm confused energy

I begin to drown
      in this familial panorama
Flashing before my eyes
     faces with various degrees of recognition
Similarly with sounds
       voices registering an array of different memories
A swirl of empathy
        or is it love
     lifts me off my feet and I float
     to wherever it takes me

I drive south
     away from the bones of my brothers
      from the bones of parents
I have done this often
     but this time feels different

The road
      the scenery
             a blank
Glazed eyes search the way ahead
A tactless wind buffets the car
      blows family ghosts into my head

      South

      I drive
          south

A bloke I know

He chooses words diffidently
       as if picking ripening plums
           from a tree
His watery eyes   slackening mouth belie
       his firm opinions
           explanations for this
            even for that
Observations range wide and wild
       they emerge tortuously slowly
but they emerge stubbornly strong

His trusty walking stick ensures
       he goes where he wants to go
He goes his way
       nobody else's

Today his way is into this sanctuary
       a frequent shelter
Others are there
       but none see him
       each too occupied with a special companion
Quickly he finds one wanting a partner

The release is instant
       release from family
           from those called friends
       from all the details
       all the demands of daily life

The need to nourish his partner
                    tugs at him
He thrusts a loaded card into its throat
feeding it fifty dollars
            it will feed him something in return
The relationship thrives
The world around them shrinks

There is just him
            him and his machine

Kookaburras

Kookaburras greet
the first gentle signs of light
with raucous chorus
welcoming loud the new day
with full-throated approval.

Pontius Pilate

for now has nothing on me
as I wash my hands
time after time through the day
and my conscience the clearer.

Umbilical matters

Local-grown navel oranges
        beam from supermarket shelves
     broadcasting a little more sunshine
into our May-shortened days

In the ancient world
     for Greeks
         sunny Delphi –
     home of the wisest oracles –
     was the navel of Mother Earth

Eagerly important men
     from so many countries
         sought there the advice
     of umbilical-bound seers
Today their voices dampened
     by the drone of tourist buses

Navels were where babies came from
     kids believed in pre-enlightened days
Could still be true
     for fathers of my generation
shouldered away from imminent birth-scenes
by formidable matrons
     devoid of sunshine
         or Delphic aura
     You'll get a phone call

Brains crust

I've seen MRI images of my brain
        In one
                too many black spots
        when black spots are not so good
but not bad for a brain of this age

Another image
                too many white spots
        when white spots are not so good
but not bad for a brain of this age

But no image shows what to do at night
        when I want to slip the brain
                        into neutral gear

Instead
        off it goes
                sniffing into recesses
                        labelled
                                unhappy memories
        or into others
                        labelled
                                unpleasant possibilities
                or one known as *Chez Demons*

Worse still
        in daylight
                it turns its back
                        denies me somebody's name
                                or the words of a crucial phrase

Thinks it's all right
        later on
        taking on a smart-alec mode
    until excess black spots
      or white spots
          brings it to heel
    and the cycle restarts

Algorithms aplenty

Algorithms affect our lives in so many ways
There seem to be so many more of them
                          these days
You stumble over them everywhere
There are some naughty ones among them
                          apparently
So we have to be on our guard
          but we have to be sensitive
We depend upon the good ones so much
               to keep things ticking over

Now if I only knew what an algorithm was

Tonight's the night

In the dark empty hours
        while he's cavorting
                on the other side of the planet
        we tweak the sun's nose
            re-schedule the markers
of our daily movements

Backwards or forwards?
        always a challenge
A huge marching army changes step
The weather
        irritated by our unseemly intrusion
                into nature's domain
        turns nasty

Daylight saving
        begins
    or
        ends

Cashier 83101

I fall in love with someone different
                        every day
Up to now
                        always a female

Today's turn was Cashier 83101
                        at the local supermarket
With a flourish
                        she swooped up my purchases
                        stowed them in my bag
But my heart stayed behind with her

Sometime tonight
                        it will limp home to me

Tomorrow's out there
                        lying in wait

Impotence

The old Egyptians believed
        being able to write your name
    gave power over you
I scrawl your name
        again and again
    covering every space I can find

Sadly
    the old gods
        are sleeping soundly

Anatomy of the History Wars

Historians thrust their hands
             up the backside of time
       using a colonoscopy process
              to seek out the polyps of misinformation

A group
       coming from the other extreme
       seeks enlightenment down the throat of ages past

Surely somewhere in the middle
             is an impassable divide
Yet it can be the territory
             preferred by more faint-hearted individuals
       who eschew the messiness of blood and guts
       their plastic-gloved hands ensuring controversy
             will not ruin their bland nightly dreams

Climate disaster

The sun fidgets offstage
       preparatory to his appearance
Kookaburras raucously rehearse his welcome
The view of the planet from where he floats
       is of an unsightly piece of work
      with ice caps shrivelling back
        the great sheets of water edging larger
          the swathes of greenery
             patchy and moth-eaten
Why should we be surprised
     if he doesn't show up tomorrow?

I could live here

I like this town
The people are fatter
         slower
                friendlier
Pedestrians treat the traffic lights
         with contempt
Along the languorous
      built-for-Cobb-and-Co street
every shop holds hands
      with each of its neighbours

Clinging on

This once-gentle town
        has its ambience defiled
as modern multi-wheeled monstrosities
          roar up the guts
               of its main drag

Such incessant outrages
        fail to daunt
           the loving lick
        that history bestows
          here

Watch out for workers

Small and black and strong
Fred Mac Amy Jan
Jim Sylvia Fran and Sam

It's dry outside
They're on the move
They duck this way
        and back the other

It's hot outside
        but does that matter?
Nothing here
        but something there

Tiniest crumbs
        any spilt food
                a cornucopia

I watch them at work
        across the chequered tablecloth

Mac Fran Amy Jim
Sylvia Fred Sam
        but Jan's gone missing

My Inner Territory

Behind some imaginary thick dark door
my fondest dreams lurk
Paddocks as far as the eye can see
undulating gently over short-cropped grass
Fields tolerating well-behaved fences
taut in their aesthetic harmony
The breath of the constant sun
lures a sweet scent from the grass
which is kept to the mandatory length
by jet black cattle, their unhurried movement
a metronome dictating the pace of life
in this place, a pace observed by a car
allowed to travel the congenial road draped
along the outer limit of my territory

The touch of the ages is needed here
so a falling-apart haystack still able
to raise a smile nestles away in a quiet corner
not far from where a cluster of six or seven graves
have guarded their precious contents
for more than a century

Then there are the living
Occasionally kids on bikes testing the bonds
shackling them to home in a nearby village
with a name recorded on a roadside signpost
stop to banter and question with a directness
encased in a piping echoing no adult can achieve

In competition with the cattle for the largesse
of the soil a small scatter of magpies stab
at the ground before taking respite in the branches
of one of the gum trees which oversee the territory

There has to be water somewhere:
the most elegant creek finds its way unobtrusively
conveying water of interesting qualities,
which I drink at a selected haven,
water infused with the ability
for me to conjure up a stage
 in the middle of an open paddock
where an orchestra performs its wizardry
Neither the cattle or the players mind each other's presence
a scenario replicated when the London Globe with its troupe
replaces the platform of musicians Pushing my luck
I imagine a dining room there of changeable shape
Large for a dinner party where my heroes from history attend
along with women from any era who have captured my special
interest Or a smaller size for more intimate encounters

But then the tug of real life cannot be ignored
          the need to exit through the old dark door
carrying a wish
                    a return visit
                         hovers as a possibility

Up there in the West

Identical in appearance
    ten of them
        unevenly spaced
    line up against the sky
there to the west of the town
    with feet planted on the very top
        of a woman-thigh-shaped hill
    the earth around them scorched bare
underneath a deceptive green blanket
    highlighting their mute starkness

Weird sentinels
    they pose a question
Certainly not locals
        do they protect the town
    from unearthly occidental forces?
Or are they in the employ
        of some sinister aliens
    hemming us in
        before some inevitable assault?

    Identical in appearance
    ten of them
        unevenly spaced
    line up against the sky
    a row of pine trees
        planted by some pioneer
    desperate to mark his puny existence
they stand in confused purposelessness
    oblivious to an occasional upward glance
    from the town below

Late March 2020

Before

He stands before his class
With an easy grace
confident   reassuring
he moves between the seated students

They watch
they see him

Images meld into their brains
destined to last for decades
twenty-four sets of images
each subtly different
some lasting the distance
better than others

They see   a guide   an elder brother
a parent   a welcome cousin
a coach   a friend   a joker
an inspiration   a manipulator
an Old Testament prophet
a safety net in human form

Without his knowing
emotions   experiences
are soaked into his psyche
channelled to visit his dreams
long after he has retired

After

He snatches a camera from the shelf
furious with life, angry with self
Stomach cramped with fierce distrust
facing this challenge something he must

He turns into an array of machines
his words, his image lands on their screens
screens of his students scattered around
not the voice they knew now distorted in sound

He puzzles over the role of the teacher
someone dispensing this stuff through the ether
A topic for him here left all on his own
seeds have been scattered but have they been sown?

He projects hate at the blue-suited oracle
who, emerging from his doctrinal follicle
spouts nothing but Delphic confusion
causing him, his peers, stark disillusion

Uncertainty sits a lump on his back
teach from home, or join in the pack
returning to classroom without too much fuss
another teacher thrown under a bus

Students spaced like lepers kept well apart
tension eased by sharing his heart
An ambience prevails borrowed from death row
he ignores it now to get on with the show

A long hard road lies there ahead
keep on teaching unless you are dead
Will the world as we know it still exist
when at last his work days have to desist?

It's a question he can't help but push aside
now any joy in his work has long since died

Lament for a coffee lounge owner

She rises early to ensure it's clean
scrubs tables, mops floors; coffee machines gleam
Times are much harder than they've ever been
The glum street outside more than a sad dream

Lynn fronts up for work, the best of the team
Her cheery face belies her inner doubt
If customer numbers run out of steam
she knows then she'll be well on the way out

The rest of the team victims of the drought
despite their energy, despite their care
slipped off the radar, a total blackout
accepted with a grace extremely rare

Home at night her fingers ruffle her hair
Forms demanding to be filled sit in a pile
She can do nothing but sit there and stare,
all around her feels so very hostile

Somewhere, some thing, some creature steeped in bile,
some virus-smitten god plays this cruel joke
She girds herself to face a daunting trial
knowing her life plan gone in one fell stroke

A special coffee mug

Its delicate congeniality is wrapped
                in a floral decoration
       a boronia of sturdy pink
       bearing blossoms
          at every stage
Some tightly wrapped
       prepubescent
         types
Others opening up to see
           what life holds
The recently nubile ones
          blush with defensive coyness
Those in glorious maturity
       dominating always
          unmatched always
       drawing empathy
          as such glory cannot last

       Boronia
    the word   the image
glides my memory back decades
      to a village
          concealed in bushland
profuse in boronial insistence

In my hand the vessel snuggles
                with feline warmth
A coffee dribble
                over some Joseph Banks handwriting
        settles among
                the boronia celebration

        No harm

                This is a hardy plant

Saintly egg

This morning
    I ate an egg for breakfast

After it was cooked
    it sank back onto my plate
        with its clean white cloak
            spread evenly about it
        its one golden eye
    looked up at me
        as if to say

    if this is to be my end
let it be as dignified
    and as useful as it can be

And so it proved

Harvesting apricots

I picture a woman
                her hair wrapped in a scarf
        her soulful eyes wide with concern
                she worries about her family
        what food she can garner for them
The pressure of work sears her stomach

This apricot is grasped by her fingers
        rapidly flicked into a basket
                with the speed of hand
                that is a gift that only women have
Or
however unlikely
                have her linger a second
                        hold this fruit apart
                ponder its ultimate destination
        later a dollop of jam
                cooked in Belgium

well outside her imagination
        headed for a faraway land
                she's hardly heard of
an old man
                who for her
could be from another planet
        someone who has time
                to stare at a slice
                        of toasted bread
to consider the dainty splodge
                        sitting there
        to wonder at the hands
                so far away
Hands that made this happen.

89

The best day

I love Wednesdays
        the fulcrum of the week
After the two harbingers
        Monday and Tuesday
                set about tentatively
        getting the week started
           it's rock-solid Wednesday
        that gives the week its flavour

Downhill after that
        on dreary Thursday
        bins out routine its most exciting prospect
Frenetic Friday obsessively occupied
        in bringing shape
           to the uncertain weekend.

Look at the names of the weekdays
        Wednesday always stands out
           with its architecturally shaped capital
Say the names aloud
        predictably all so straightforward
           except for Wednesday
        where the sounds playfully
           go their own way
        in defiance of the order of the letters

So Wednesday's independence from the power
        of grumpy old Woden is flaunted
           every time the day is spoken

If only every day could be a Wednesday

Day's kiss is bleak

Day's kiss is bleak
  damped down by thick clouds
A gentle moisture
    lubricates the two way passage
  of affection
    between sky and earth

A quiet observes
    this subtle entanglement
Trees join the vigil

A breath
  ephemeral
    from who knows where
  disturbs this arrangement
    but soon flees the scene

The sticky feet of time
  confuses all
    who await its passing

Even birds respect the silence

Death of a Dutch Iris

The tour of duty nears its end
Blue cosseting golden spills –
    the conjunction of colours
radiates fragile beauty
      destined to live on
          in secret places
despite acid time's encroaching shrivel

Winter

A bad haircut of trees edge the street
    spilling their long shadows
        Other trees stand to attention
            in prickly nakedness
Fine mountain mist
    a tawdry curtain
        spreads its untidiness over all
The world shrugs into itself
        thrusts its hands deep into its pockets
    the air bites those whose feet punish the footpath
Despite the movement of traffic
    a stillness clamps over the wider tableau
An impatient meanness ingrains into the cells
        of living matter
    our souls
        like unhappy flowers
            devoid of sufficient sunshine
    curl up into themselves
    Winter turns into a time
        for struggling to survive
            putting off hopes
    to give up caring
A time to employ a jaundiced eye
        for the long wait
            for spring's supposed coming

Southern Solstice

Today is longer than yesterday
                by a split second or so
We are being sucked
                        towards indolent days
                that wade through heat and glare
                        numb the brain as it soaks
                                in festive inanity
                furnish public places with eyefuls
                        of bare skin
long legs   midriffs   shoulders
        buttocks
                        play-acting at being accommodated
        in make-believe shorts
All while the calendar changes its uniform

Today is longer than yesterday
                we drift towards future events
                to be written by History's thick clumsy fingers
                in ink composed of blood
                        seasoned in pestilence and greed
Terrifying   tsunami   tempests   seismic
                                                assaults
                                fire
                        flood
                drought
poised to write
                their malodorous stories in heinous hieroglyphs
across the planet's
                already ravaged visage

Today is longer than yesterday
the beginning of a drag
towards year's clamorous end

One less for us to endure
The number in the credit column shrinks

Trees in August

Leafless trees stand aghast
          at their condition
     yearn for fulfilment
a sense of something stirring within
       a bursting out of inner self
              releasing identity into countless buds

Content then at the potential
         bundled into cone-shaped outpourings
           of energy and colour

Time to breathe in the brisk air
         savour the glory days to come.

A sometime feeling

Flat days
        flat ways
                with barely a wrinkle
such smoothness accelerating
                their ease of moving by
        without being marked
                by particular joy or sadness
leaving in their slipstream
        a merest hint of grim satisfaction
that they keep recurring

Sloth

Sloth
shamed
deadly sin
by moralists
but what else is there on a wet Sunday
except drink coffee and read newspapers
if you decide
not to go
to your
church

Tanka

On Sundays he leaves
his five dogs locked in his house
while he goes to Mass
unaware their loud barking
turns neighbours away from God.

God

God
up there
on his throne
watching the world
while we scratch around for an existence
having to obey a heap of his laws
under the threat
of being
sent to
Hell

Tanka

The reaper's fingers
searching for a fatal flaw
relentlessly probe
every possible aspect
of this my aged body.

De-ceased

These days
            they don't say he died
        but he passed

        Passed?
With distinction?
        Or honours
a credit
        or just a pass?

Such awards can be insensitive

This my bed

Nine hours every night
                    coupled to this place
it wraps my life into even-sized slices

Darkness insulates secret weaknesses
           the rumpled blanket a confessional

Dark and wakefulness lures forth
                    a bouquet of strangest mix
           hopes
                    fears
                         clever ideas

Slivers of different memory flare up
                    before fleeing

Pillow   sheet   doona
           soak into their fibre and feathers
                    the night sounds I share
           the aggressive charge of goods train
                    bluster of stormy wind
                         early morning bird anarchy
           More intimately
                    unconscious whispers
           groans   sneezes

The nearness of a cherished companion
                    cannot cloak a message hammering
                         through the dark wakefulness
           In this life
                    you are alone

Morning demands action
    the tangle of dreams pushed aside
        sheets and blanket straightened
           to unnatural orderliness

Night's chaos banished
        ignored
  until darkness returns

    A shared game of pretence

Also set aside for now
    the bed-and-me communication
        on the possible how and when
    of a shared
        final caress

Sleep

Every night
                 like a walk in the dark house
         where horizons shift disconcertingly
revealed in gaps
              between moving blinds
                  of different intensity
Every footfall lands on a shaky surface
        every helpful object
               just
     out
           of
     reach

Morning sunlight brings no comfort
          just a temporary respite
      a harbinger of another night
           swooping to encompass all.

Youth and Asia

I'm not reaching for it yet
but I wouldn't mind
              having it in my kitbag
It could get a bit rough
         not so far down the track

Insanitus Contentious

Oh, it's good to be mad
      to be able
           to kick off
                the pinching shoes
           of drab rationality

Shrinking of paradise

cinema
                main street coffee shop
                   sun deck
     playhouse
          son's beach house
library
          concert hall
     nearby park

all these
     have gathered up their skirts
crowded into this small room
cheerless room
where he is fed
showered
visited
Which he seldom leaves
When he leaves
where he craves to return to
Where he sleeps
     dreams
wakes
     and wonders
Where he sleeps
     dreams
wakes
     and waits

Pandemic curse

It strikes the old, it strikes the young
Away from families, away from friends
they feel abandoned and very alone
In clinical isolation they await their ends

Away from families, away from friends
no one to talk to, no friendly smile to comfort
In clinical isolation they await their ends
The space-suited nurses pour out their all

No one to talk to, no friendly smile to comfort
the saddest way to leave this life
The space-suited nurses pour out their all
At this stage you're all on your own

The saddest way to leave this life
They feel abandoned and very alone
At this stage, you're all on your own
The struck down young, the struck down old.

Across the way

Quizzed through a grilled window
      the grey-clad Gib* edges horizontally
            in a gentle dragon-backed undulate
                  dominating over layers of nearby

treetops

The basic visual never changes
The back-lighting varies
            sun
cloud   mist
         sweeping rain

Take your choice
They carve up passing periods of time
      into more digestible slices
           ingested from a hospital bed

* Mount Gibraltar

110

Covid victim

Waking hours spent reciting old poems
Prayers he considers go up in smoke
Dredging memories from his different homes
but confined here at one fell stroke

Not a familiar figure since he last awoke
except kindly nurses in their space age gear
It's ages since he smiled, ages since he spoke
he has plenty to think about, plenty to fear

His mouth and nose imprisoned, no room for a tear
he welcomes gas forcibly entering his chest
He bundles memories, fights to keep them clear
but his sins haunt him, none of them confessed

Like a knight nearing the end of his quest
he scans the horizon, he ponders his past
His life nearly ended, it's time for his rest
his fist tightly clenched, he breathes his last

For Tom

In eulogy mode
        I called you brother
      but no brother of mine could speak French
               with such flair
     or play musical instruments
          with such gusto
     or bestride the English language with such élan

You cocked a snook
              at the privileged and greedy
Cocked a snook!
        I can hear you laugh
      at such cack-handed irreverence

You seized life by the scruff of the neck
      and kicked it around
         with sheer delight
When it turned its back on you
          you faced the inevitable
       with the same courage and dignity
    shown by the young men
        near whose graves in northern France
   you often played the Last Post
       to such haunting effect

Since you left us

         life has dusted its pants
     looked around ruefully
There is less spring in its step

          its appearance is tattered

Nothing will ever be the same
Trance-like we plod along in life's footsteps

Nothing ever the same

This business of dying

Of course when we are nearly at that stage ourselves
     our parents are dead aren't they?
Was there when my dad died
Family
          bearing tears and rosary beads
     and sleepwalking down an unknown path
          crowded around the hospital bed
Saw Dad encoffined afterwards
     but it really wasn't him
About as relevant as the cicada shell
     found on late summer's ground

Was heading there when it was my mother's turn
Never made it in time
     cars clustered around the family home
          told me all I wanted to know

Watching the dying
     the waiting
   is not the greatest spectator sport
   added to the fact
some of us want to exit stage left
      unobserved
As the crucial moment crept closer
     Voltaire dismissed his vulture-hovering
         priest companion
     with a *Go Leave me in peace*

Tom
      my Francophile friend
              slipped the knot of life
          while the night was full-bellied
      and his family dreaming plans
        of future hospital visits

While we may have abandoned this life
      leaving just our discarded bits and bones behind
          the sad circus continues back here

Oh I remember the eulogies
      the homely ones with words smeared
              on quivering paper
      the practised ones
          clinical in their thoroughness
      the others
        blurted out between tearful pauses
all recreating a tidied picture of a lost past

Then the cemeteries
      one where a subterranean network
          of DNA's resembling mine
      lies in wait for additions

          And so it goes

Or so it ends

Acknowledgements

The following poems have been previously published:
'2B or other'; 'Ophelia drowning' in *Burrow*
'Backyard rebirth'; 'Southern solstice' in *Eureka Street*
'To origins and back'; 'Strange fruit: different types, different
places' in *BlazeVOX*
'Pontius Pilate' in *Eucalypt Journal*
'Into the fray with LBJ' in *I Protest*
'Mountainous aspirations' in *Mountain Secrets*
'Infants school playground'; 'Algorithms aplenty';
'Grammarian to his love'; 'Tonight's the night';
The best day'; 'Death of a Dutch Iris'; 'A sometime feeling'
in *Writers Voice*
'Shrinking of Paradise' in both *Writers Voice* and *Blaze VOX*

CPSIA information can be obtained
at www.ICGtesting.com
Printed in the USA
LVHW020617270722
724372LV00013B/410